Coltrane's God

Coltrane's God

Donald Levering

For Eve —
Sister in the
CRAFT
Donald
KCMO
Sept 2017

I am grateful to the editors of the following publications, in which these poems, often in earlier versions, previously appeared:

Atlanta Review, "For a Glass Harp Player"; *Blue Rock Review,* "Ear Worm"; *The Chariton Review,* "This is Not a Song I Used to Know"; *Cottonwood Review,* "Lament from the Black Swamp"; *Culturenet.com,* "Grandpa"; *Envoi,* "The Choir of Youthful Suicides"; *Gris-Gris,* "Fiddle Fest Contestants," "A Night in Tunisia"; *Inkwell,* "The Man with the Golden Arm"; *IthacaLit,* "After Hours," Cajón Maestro," "Talking to the Octopus"; *Malpais Review,* "Hymn"; *New Press Literary Quarterly,* "Broke Down House"; *Santa Fe Literary Review,* "Before the Blues Blues"; *Stirring,* "Busker."

"Barrelhouses" was First Runner-Up for the Mark Fischer Award.

ISBN 978-0-9908047-3-4

Printed in the United States of America

RED MOUNTAIN PRESS

Santa Fe, New Mexico
www.redmountainpress.us

In the spirit of
Orlando's fiddle,
Elsie's hymnal,
and Jim's piano

ACKNOWLEDGMENTS	7
THE CHARTS	9
THE SOUNDING	18
FOR A GLASS HARP PLAYER	20
BEFORE THE BLUES BLUES	21
BARRELHOUSES	24
COLTRANE'S GOD ADMONISHES	26
A NIGHT IN TUNISIA	28
ABANDONED SILVER MINE	30
THIS IS NOT A SONG I USED TO KNOW	32
GRANDPA	34
FIDDLE FEST CONTESTANTS	36
MUSICIANS	38
TALKING TO THE OCTOPUS	40
CAJÓN MAESTRO	42
BUSKER	44
YOGA TEACHER IN LILONGWE TRAFFIC	45
THE MAN WITH THE GOLDEN HORN	48
BROKE DOWN HOUSE	50
NEPTUNE FESTIVAL	52
LAMENT FROM THE BLACK SWAMP	54
THE CHOIR OF YOUTHFUL SUICIDES	56
HYMN	58
AFTER HOURS	59
EAR WORM	60
LINER NOTES	62

Acknowledgments

Many thanks to Daniel Bohnhorst, Debbi Brody, Stephen Bunch, Sheila Cowing, Robyn Hunt, Wayne Lee, John Lofflin, Denise Low, Argos MacCullum, David Markwardt, Joan Mitchell, Gary Moody, Mary Morris, Kim Parko, Elizabeth Raby, Robert Ricci, Barbara Rockman, Michael Scofield, Jane Shoenfeld, and Leslie Ullman, who have provided ongoing support and insight for my poetry. Special thanks to Susan Gardner for her superb editing and design work and to Devon Ross, who supported her in this project, and to them both for believing in this book.

Sound in darkness. Dreamtime punctuated by heartbeats. Mother's breathing, Mother's voice through flesh.

Whale song from the age of the walking whales comes into womb time. A whale surfaces in a cloud of spume, calls to a wounded human, mends flesh and spirit, melds sound and light ("The Sounding"). Whale song reverberations lift from ocean to mountains, tunnel through long Tibetan dharma trumpets or Swiss alphorns.

Sound performs better in water than air. Spiritualists conjure ghostly voices by skimming rims of water glasses ("For a Glass Harp Player"). The sound of water is music to humans. In a Japanese Zen garden, falling water trips a cavalcade of pure tones. Beneath the hectic streets of Istanbul, stone stairs lead down to a vast, cool room, a Byzantine cistern with walkways cobbled from Roman ruins. Colored lights play across the pools of water. Telemann's bright trumpet concerto is piped through suspended speakers. Resplendence reverberates off walls and water.

Music evokes emotion, activates memory. I love to read the story of how a klezmer band transformed an Alzheimer's ward in a Jewish rest home from zombie clutch to rooms of joyful reminiscence. Love to listen to Bessie Smith belting out her blues ("Before the Blues Blues") to dance myself silly to *Mustang Sally* or *Brown Sugar*, to get aerobic *Burning Down the House*. I am enraptured listening to the perfection of a Bach concerto, stirred by the exorcism of the Ramayana Monkey Chant. Why not make poems out of the experience?

Writing about, say, *Mood Indigo* differs from doing a musical cover of it. The poet picks from a different toolbox than the Duke. Verbal language can be so deft in its pinging of the neocortex and making of meanings. Music also can engage intellect, yet it immerses, too, at a sonic level, through its plenitude of notes and beats, ostinatos, trumpet mutes, wah-wah pedals, bells, falsettos and fortissimos. Your poem about a song is not a song unless you sing it, don't mean a thing if it don't swing.

Not a musician, what do I know about music? I know what any outsider to an art knows: how it affects me. How it makes me close my eyes and follow its labyrinthine melodies, its percussive starbursts and rainbow harmonies. How I want to hum or sing along with it or jiggle my knee or get up and dance. How it chimes my nostalgia with sentiments I dare not allow to intrude into a poem.

It's the wanna-be musician in me that identifies this book's poems as "tracks" and this commentary as "The Charts." Those parent-paid piano lessons never "took." The excuse I've told myself: my editing impulse was too strong to let me play through mistakes. What works well for perfecting a written poem is deadly to musical performance.

To become a performing musician is to repeat difficult feats. Practice until your (pick one or more) lips, fingers, voice, brain are beyond tired and sore, until muscle memory takes hold and musical thoughts are embodied in muscles and nerves ("Musicians"). How freeing it must be to achieve fluency in music's language of emotion with your breath or voice or fingers or feet. I once witnessed John Hartford simultaneously fiddle, clog, and sing a song with complicated lyrics he had written. The man was made of music. Then there was blind Rahsaan Roland Kirk, playing three horns in harmony at once.

Music was introduced to me bundled with religion. To a young person, hymns can be ponderous vessels of joy, sorrow, submission, or transfiguration. They can dispirit or uplift long after the cord to their creed is cut ("Hymn"). For some young people, unfortunately, the sustenance offered by music and religion are not enough to keep them in life's dance ("The Choir of Youthful Suicides").

Choir practice became more discouragement than uplift. My voice early began the change of puberty. The children's choir director was fascinated with my changing voice. He'd stoop beside me for what seemed hours as I struggled to find the octave where my voice could blend with the other cherubs. It was a frightful, squeaky growl. I imagined my voice sounded like the saurian devil on the stained-glass pane I'd stare at while the director's ear hovered nearby. It was as if some clue to the origins of music were in that painful straining between soprano and baritone.

By mutual consent, I left the children's choir and never found my way into a choral group. Later forays into guitar and back to piano confirmed my talent lay elsewhere than in music.

My paternal grandfather was an itinerant musician in his younger years, fiddling his way around work camps in the West ("Grandpa"). Often I wish I could have heard him play. Letters of those who knew him rave about his bodacious fiddle playing. I inherited a photograph of him as a winner at a fiddle festival ("Fiddle Fest Contestants"), as well as an inbred love of old-time country and bluegrass music. Natural, then, to include in this book references to country songs of snubbed lovers and laments of guilt and regret ("This is Not a Song I Used to Know"). I'm easily prompted to cue up Hank Williams or Merle Haggard, turn the dial to Patsy Cline, or cross over from country into Ray Charles' *Crying Time* or Billie's weeping willow.

Among my four brothers, one was truly musical, and Jim still delights at the piano. His resounding *This Ole House* was a theme song of our romper room youth ("Broke Down House"). But don't read strict autobiography into every note of these poems. A poem's "facts" are not necessarily verifiable outside the poem. That is why I have Chet Baker playing the sound track of *The Man with the Golden Arm*. Baker exemplifies a troubled trumpeter far better than actual studio musician Shorty Rogers ever could. As Muddy Waters bends notes on his guitar for effect, so literal truth can be bent for art's truth.

Always I loved to listen to music. I was in junior high when brother Bob turned me on to Beethoven's fifth symphony. Other romantics followed — Tchaikovsky, Rachmaninoff. I had thought "classical" music was stuffy, but these composers swept me away. Then Bob brought home a quarter-inch-thick vinyl record from Bombay with a white dog on the red label whose ear was cocked to a gramophone. New worlds of tonal scale and rhythm unfolded as the little dog chased around ragas by Ali Akbar Khan.

The Beatles spawned a wave of creativity in the transistor pop music I internalized. Rock and blues came along in college. Friends helped me transition from jamming Grateful Dead to jazz, thus opening other aural vistas. I'd never heard anything as mysterious and trippy as Miles Davis' *Bitches Brew* and Charles Lloyd's and Keith Jarrett's *Forest Flower.*

Among the decibels of traffic horns and harsh machine noise, how welcome are interludes of music in the streets! The ancient art of buskering flourishes ("Busker") with sidewalk electric guitarists and subway station cello sonatas, with arias stopping foot traffic on the avenues and one-man rattletrap bands a-clatter under dripping awnings ("Cajon Maestro").

Improvisation continues after the last set, in the keyboard player's walk-up flat or singers' scat echoed in a tram tunnel or, in warm weather, in that quintessential communion of urban jazz, a street corner jam ("After Hours").

In Malawi, one group of boys performs for motorists songs about the mice they catch at dawn for their mothers to fry for travellers to buy. True roots music — the Mice Boys play a guitar made from a cooking-oil tin box attached to a tree limb. (I could dwell for months in The Musical Instrument Museum in Phoenix). In our plugged-in world, the universal sound of *OM* can travel from Calcutta ashrams to Lilongwe traffic jams ("Yoga Teacher in Lilongwe Traffic").

Oliver Sacks writes in *Musicophilia* about "ear worms"— not parasites, but strains of music that persist inside the brain, those songs that get "stuck in your head." How is it possible that Chuck Berry or Mendelssohn or Zulu thumb-piano tunes override or accompany our thoughts and perceptions? That they come unbidden is so uncanny, and, to some of us, at full orchestration and length, adds to the enthrallment ("Ear Worm"). We can be haunted by a blues tune that conjures the memory of an ex-wife ("Abandoned Silver Mine"), or a bluegrass breakdown recalled can bring back a sad man who once mastered its banjo fingering ("Lament from the Black Swamp").

Musical ideas can come to us in dreams. Before he died in an insane asylum, Robert Schumann dreamt that the ghost of Franz Schubert dictated a musical theme to him. Schumann subsequently used this theme in several compositions, including his work for piano called *Ghost Variations*. It's not surprising to me that shortly after his death, my bipolar brother appeared in my dream urging me to orchestrate an entire festival in honor of Neptune, replete with, among other extravagances, tuba solos and Eric Dolphy honking his bass clarinet ("Neptune Festival").

I feel lucky that poets get to do such presumptuous things as claiming to speak in the voice of another man's god ("Coltrane's God Admonishes"). Yet it seems not far-fetched to propose that Coltrane was somehow guided in his astounding transformations. Musically, he transmuted hard bop into a unique style with original forms, creating what came to be known as "sheets of sound" and "Coltrane [chord] changes." He took *My Favorite Things* from a saccharin show tune and morphed it into an existential hullabaloo. He transformed the tragedy of the racist bombing of the Birmingham Baptist Church into the moving requiem, *Alabama*. On the personal level, he reported that God spoke to him during his cold-turkey heroin withdrawal, granting him release from the drug's shackles in order to use music to raise his listeners' awareness. The message that Coltrane's god seems to have conveyed was to keep searching and changing and growing in music and spirit. By his death at age 40, Coltrane embraced a universal, inclusive understanding of God beyond all "isms," and his music was its unbound expression.

The Sounding

On her rooftop deck under stars in high desert,
among cricket chirp, bat click, and swallow titter,
    the composer, nursing her surgery,
    calmly begins her story
from the summer place far to the north.

There, too, she'd been seated on a deck,
only there it was day and the view was of seaway.
She was reading Meister Eckhart's
    sermon on nature's abundance.
Through the meister's words there surfaced

three pulses followed by a rising, unfamiliar sound.
    She looked up from her book to search
    for its source, and spied
the curving form of a breaching minke whale.

She sprang to the railing, watched it rise again,
    and listened.
From deeper than the ache in her chest
    came her call across water.

Again the whale rose from the depths,
twisting to expose its white belly,
        and intoned.
Once more she gathered breath from her core
and called, and again
        the minke breached and sounded.

Back here, she returns to her chair.
A long while we listen
        to the sea of nightspeak
        pinging from the healing deep.

For a Glass Harp Player

Marianne Davies (1744-1816)

Later the leaded glass was blamed for your melancholic decline, the tortured agitation, tremors like swallows' flight, and audio hallucinations. But in your glory, Marianne, how your audience was lifted to the arch that spans the celestial river, how the glasses rang their otherworldly strains, as your fingertips, dipped in rainwater, circled the crystal.

Vibratos from your instrument disoriented listeners, seeming both near and distant, like something inner deemed to arise from outside the psyche. Your skimming fingers conjured that realm across the bridge where seraphs dwell, suffused in music of pure water, ethereal, almost beyond human hearing.

With tones so delicate and clear, this silvered medium of yearned-for contact with the dearly departed served your sister spiritualists, who learned from you the magic of trembling moistened glasses. They, too, succumbed to nervous madness, for who could long absorb such eerie timbres, who could play forever among the leaden choruses of the dead?

Before the Blues Blues

Before Bessie Smith's *Jelly Roll Man*
It began
Before the cotton gin and bathtub gin
Before tuberculosis racked Otis Spann

There were no black keys on pianos
No senators of color
And everyone was of the pure
Grey race before the blues

Nobody studied war before the blues
None were sent to the back of the bus
No one ordered *Lift that bail*
This was before Bo Jangles danced in jail

Before W. C. Handy's *Memphis*
And Jimmy Reed's first fix
Before dirty snow drifts in Chicago
And Robert Johnson's jealous poisoning

Before the blues Jehovah was color-blind
And lovers remained faithful
The baby called Rock 'n' Roll
Had yet to be born

Not a one spoke in tongues
Before the blues no scat
No rap no hip-hop no slam
No cool cats jammin' before the blues

Before *Old Man River* and Muddy Waters
Before Jim Crow laws and Black Crow bottles
When husbands had no cause to wail
There's another mule kickin' in my stall

Sherman hadn't burned his way through Dixie
This was way before boogie-woogie
Before slide trombones and stride piano
Before Ray Charles lost his sight

No one's shoes were full of holes
And nobody was missing a soul
None had indoor plumbing
There was no underground railroad

There were no mouth harps or electric guitars
Saxophones merely marched in military bands
Before the blues no blind octoroons
Crooned on corners in Baton Rouge

No flatted thirds and sevenths
Before the blues
The twelfth bar didn't signal another round
This was before "colored" water fountains

Before Juneteenth and Billie Holiday
Before the *Amistad* and "Moses" Tubman
Before anyone dreamed of bending notes
Before Reverend King had his dream

There was no Langston Hughes
No lonely avenues in East St. Louis
No hangovers no remorse
Only bright dawns before the blues

Barrelhouses

Sounds like they'd be buildings made of curved boards
fitted like barrel staves, but barrelhouses
were only round in how blues men rotated through
on their circuit of turpentine camps,

how raucous songs rolled out in twelve-bar rounds,
how workers cycled from crushing labor, woozy fumes
            to beer and rollicking rhythms,
                        reefer-rising spirits,
and back to hungover piecework,

how pianos were rolled on flatbeds down back roads
to fill these boozy sheds where a trumpet would trill
or saxophone squall, or mouth harp would wail
or banjo plink above the piano's striding bass,

how the likes of Jelly Roll Morton and Meade Lux Lewis
wore grooves in the keys, how these barns
racked with barrels of bad bourbon would bulge
with romping rounders and river-hipped mamas,

would swell with smoke and sweat
            and *Pinetop's Boogie-Woogie*
from the rapid hands of Memphis Slim
            or Champion Jack,

or an unknown handyman would jam
          within these ramshackle frames
for field hands and dealers, roustabouts
          and flimflam men,

would rumble through *Black Wolf Blues,* only stopping
to knock back boilermakers perched on the piano,
the hoarse chorus of *All My Money's Gone*
ringing across stubble fields in early morning,

before the camps tapped out all the pine trees'
          turpentine sap,
before barrelhouse boards warped with rain
          and the weight of busted schemes,
collapsed beside highways
          and were gleaned for firewood,
the pianos rolling from roadhouses

to urban bars, the workers dispersed into dust storms,
bread queues, world wars, the blues drifting
into East St. Louis, South Chicago, up to Harlem,
over to Paris and Liverpool,

the barrelhouses coming round.

Coltrane's God Admonishes

You were bestowed the huge brass hook of the sax
Now you bring them a ballad for balm
The *Sentimental Mood* they can hum
But before they become too relaxed
Overblow some off-the-charts chord

So they know whose music breathes through you

Your whispering reed of love in *Naima*
Was not pitched to your wife alone
Her worship was rehearsal
For I heard you sixteen times intone
A Love Supreme

Before feeling your way to me with your horn

Recall my joy before you inject
Once more the white noise
Remember psalms and clapping spirituals
Along with the gospel according to Bird
Call and response of cicadas and frogs

Before the church in Birmingham was bombed

Who led you to Pharaoh and Monk
Call me Cosmic Improvisation
Buzz-in-the-Reeds or Sustaining Vibration
I'm your freedom from the white poison
Your *Blue Train* conductor

Your chorus of desegregation

I hear you praying to me however you play
Offer them their *Favorite Things, Body and Soul*
Then give them your changes, sheets of sound
Shiver them with your howling *OM*
Blister their ears with arpeggios

Repeat forever with variations

A Night in Tunisia

is not the name of the stone-&-timber
former silver mine jammed with grizzled hippies,
feisty dykes, buckled bikers, jazz-&-black-tar

junkies who can point to the stool
where last week one of their own
slumped into his rush and never rallied.

Packs of dogs patrol the bar, as if we'd arrived
in some dusty African outpost
and not a revived mining town

of the American West called Madrid,
which you just mispronounced in your head;
the residents stress syllable one like an upbeat.

The band is wrapping *Scrapple from the Apple*
as *los perros* squabble over scraps.
Near the Mineshaft Tavern sign a fan

calls out Dizzy's tune; the group dismisses
their set list to confer about
Tunisia's key and chord changes.

They strike up a long introduction,
cool & meditative, like Miles Davis
nodding off on smooth steel rails to Copenhagen,

before the tempo changes and we ride
the syncopation train to Tunis.
Why this combo turned up here

with their East Coast *nuevo* bop
the locals are too stoned to grasp
is not danceable,

weaving cobra-charmer arms in slow mo
to sax prestissimo.
How the house percussionist hustles

to keep pace; how the keyboard player
turns *Tunisia* into a revelation.
How the lanky bass gambols through it all,

even when the whacked-out hooker
mounts the stage and shakes her bazooms.
Shrill whistles penetrate applause and cheers,

but the band has rolled on into *Perdido*,
standing before the maw of the played-out mine,
a breeze from within blowing through them.

ABANDONED SILVER MINE

Here to lose my story in history,
to walk off my divorce, but the scurry
at my feet perturbs like heaving earth.
Some drumbeat in the earth has stirred
tarantulas to desert their burrows.

I've heard they migrate through
these autumn afternoons to find mates;
then males scramble to escape
becoming partners' prey.
Without remorse or guilt they flee.

Thousands of them rustle through
the tailings of this tapped-out mine
in hills of cactus, juniper, and pinyon.
When I pause to listen, inside my brain
for the hundredth time today,

the haunted Robert Johnson wails
"Hell Hound On My Trail,"
Blues falling down like rain,
Hot foot powder all around my door,
I got to keep on movin'.

The placard at the brink
tells of murders over this claim.
This pit that swallowed miners' hopes
now ingests a desert sprinkle.
Looking down,

my pupils take forever to open
to the blackness within the pit,
and there my ex-wife's face
seems to hover, waiting.
I got to keep on movin'.

This is Not a Song I Used to Know

Not one of those cheerful reels
Grandpa played on his fiddle
for weddings. More like *Tom Dooley,*
or *Down in the Heart Country.*
In this crooning I might long
for the bittersweet harmony
of Kentucky's blue moon

rising over Bill Monroe's cold body.
This song is not the trilling
of the red-winged blackbird
outside the window of our first home.
I wish I knew which song to hum
under the bruised moon of divorce,
or how to whistle the waltz out the door.

Am I the brother to the walking bass
that is father of this ballad?
Is this my strawhatted band
in double time, my mandolin picker
stitching his wounded heart?
Is this my voice drowned at sea
with the *Wildwood Flower's* darling?

Strike up your joyful gospel
elsewhere, I'll brood inside
this lament for withered love,
blind to passion's cardinals
and pining for Doc Watson's
twelve-string chords
that could move mountains.

How many years of marriage down,
and she who once joined my refrains
is as gone as my scratched vinyl
of the Clinch Mountain Boys.
Oh, where is my Mother
Maybelle Carter, where
is her heart's lullaby?

Grandpa

It takes a worried man
to sing a worried song

So green was Grandma's thumb,
even in the Mojave she grew
bumper crops of apricots and plums.
Her merchant savvy turned
her husband's farmwork blisters
into stacks of greenbacks.
Mother told me so
and so it's true.

She said that Grandpa'd rambled
in his youth across the West.
He'd lingered in a camp
beside the Colorado River
where families slept in cardboard shacks,
waiting for the telegram from Washington
to give the order
to set the blasting caps for Hoover dam.

While he'd waited for his job
he honed his fiddle's voice.
He found some men with banjos
and guitars, and they joined
a pair of sisters whose crooning
took on everybody's longing.
They blended all their voices
and turned that shantytown to song.

That telegram kept not arriving.
And Grandpa got so hungry
he ate rattlesnakes, got so chilled
he couldn't finger his fiddle.
So he bundled his belongings,
hopped a freight to Arizona
where he helped raise a trestle
with his fiddle and his worried songs.

Fiddle Fest Contestants

Kansas City, March 22, 1928

Half a year before the crash
that scattered armies of the dispossessed,
my dad's father poses with bow in hand
among his kindred with their fiddles,
mandolins, guitars, and single balalaika,
ready to be plucked from their era
to rest within a frame on my mantel.

A hooded box's panoramic lens
had curved the view to take in
the ballroom's width, so the long rows
of music makers, armed with instruments,
bulge to form a phalanx against
the tedium of farm and factory.

With worsted suits, white shirts, and bow ties,
the players seem less like rowdy rounders,
though the front row gal in flapper's garb,
hand around her banjo's frets,
invites me to guess
it was as much a party as a contest.

Grandfather sits with his fiddle in his lap
and winner's ribbon on his vest,
this man I never knew
but heard had roamed around the West.

Now hear their mingled repertoire
of reels, jigs, and breakdowns,
polkas, rags, and waltzes
merge into a frieze of sound,
as time is circular
and music goes in rounds,
and songs are handed down.

Musicians

You practice till your lips grow numb

To give the people dance you trapped
the antelope's pulse in a drum
sealed with the skin of a python
rumba   rain   fandango   hornpipe

You caught a cricket too
minuet   lindy hop   watusi
along with osprey wing beats   clatter of caribou
morris   tarantella   polonaise

You dwell in the bell of a tuba

To show where to place your fingers
and your breath
ant-like figures
crawl across staves
away from the signs of the clef

You practice till you can play unconscious

To repeat your performances
millions of miles of tape
were wound onto spools

immense vats of plastic
have been pressed into flapjacks of tunes

You clack and clack your castanets

With you the oboe plays the cobra
the Andean flute soars like a condor
the monkey cranks the barrel organ
spittle is shaken from mouth harp
catgut is strung on the fiddle

You practice till you snap your last drumstick

In you our ancestors endure
by your droning bagpipes
by your strutting cellos
your overtones
and diminuendos

After blind auditions with blistered fingers
After improbable improvisations lung sore
With strained vocal cords with tendinitis
After innumerable repetitions

You finish the score
with the grin of getting it right

Talking to the Octopus

Let me introduce you to a human,
Trentacosta — ilk of Krupa, Cobham.
Think you share some things in common.

When John is swinging, he seems to brandish
doubled arms and legs that carry on
independent of his thought.

He has extensions for his limbs to tap
the skins, brushes swishing surf-like,
kick drums making thunder.

John can rattle seven-eighths
and shift the meter
as quick as you change colors.

You might wonder what is this thing
called *music* that he does.
With your three hearts, maybe you can fathom

love that's at its bottom.
We've noticed that your eight arms
don't need your brain to find your mates.

So why does Trentacosta keep the beat
for the guy who blows through reeds,
why measure time for the organist

making swells of sound?
Your tentative response tells me
I may as well be squirting clouds of ink.

Although you're clever and vision's keen,
you have no organs for receiving sound.
I'll have to turn my words to Braille

that octopi can read, for none of this
about the maestro Trentacosta
will make sense

without your sense of touch.

Cajón Maestro

Cloudbursts dampen Lima without thunder.
To punctuate the gentle patter,
this boy was born who buskered
solo as percussion band
before he was discovered
by the trumpeter who raised him
late in middle age to the national stage.

His palms still stinging from the last number,
he stands up from his box drum to cradle
the long lower jawbone of a donkey.
With a stick he scrapes across the teeth
to set them buzzing in their sockets
and sharply strikes the mandible,
alternating buzz and clack
beneath strummed guitar and trumpet runs.

Lowering the donkey jaw,
he straps on the *cajonita*,
the church collection box
converted to a drum he hits
with his stick while clapping
its hinged lid, a syncopated clatter
for the hen-and-rooster dance.

The band pauses; couples clear
the floor for everyone to watch
his Zapateo dance,
clicking heels and toe taps, hands
in rapid whapping of his thighs,
the complicated signature
of a man who's younger than his years.

Busker

Scuffing shoes skirt you as you strum in the drizzle.
Many faces turn away. But a few pause midstream
for a bar or two of sad ballad.

Another lovesick song seizes you,
twitching your fingers on the strings,
swelling your voice.

Your pick has scratched a splintered star
in the body of your sorry guitar, a hole
over your heart enlarged by strumming

where each chord homes to, where your lore
as fool to saintly whore replays.
Sure, it is not really you clogging commerce

on this slick Dublin sidewalk
with coins clinking in your open case.
You dwell in a more ardent age

entangled here by mistake.
Still, there are those passersby
who stop to listen in the rain.

Yoga Teacher in Lilongwe Traffic

The light has changed
                    but no one's moving —
five lanes crowded into two,
and someone's broken down.
Bad form to be late
                    for my own class.

Nothing I can do
but listen to a taped lesson
                    while I'm waiting.

Breathe into the tight places.

There's the holdup,
in front of that oil burner.
The scrap-metal men
will have harvested that car
before its owner returns.

Could've been me
                    with this rattletrap.

Observe the difference between the two sides.

I hear voices —

"We wake before sunrise
out to the fields we go
where the mice are slow
from all-night eating rice."

— It's the mice boys.
I've seen them before, chanting
as they thread between traffic
selling fried mice stuck on sticks.

Hold downward dog five breaths.

Tasty, cheap protein — hope
they don't sell out before they get to me.
Toast and tea breakfast seems hours ago.

If your spine is feeling more flexible
fold your legs over into plow.

Look how they trade their mice for money
and still keep drumming plastic water jugs
while they sing five-part harmony —

"We watch out for mambas
also hunting for mice!
Umm, how our mamas
fry them up with spice."

OM has to come from your core.
Your exhale should equal your inhale.

Still stuck
behind that belching truck.
I'll wave the boys over
and buy four.
If I miss this class,
I won't make the rent.

No comparisons, no judgment.

The Man with the Golden Horn

All I recall are fragments of its plot,
sitting with my older brother Bob
in the back of the Dickens Theatre,
and the illumined motes that led
from the window behind us to the screen,
the room suffused in yellow light.
Dealing cards, the man's damp arm
shone like the golden calf
in *The Ten Commandments*.
I'd never heard of heroin,
as the man injected his arm
with what made the scene go soft
for the span of an understated score
played by Chet Baker.

So the film has come to be
about a *golden horn*,
an instrument played so sweet
in Baker's strung out hands
the world went golden.
This was '55, when war euphoria
was wearing off.
The big dance bands had shrunk
to moody combos,
and my idols were athletes,
so this man's arm must have flung baseballs.

He'd have been the strikeout king
with a fat contract
and buxom babes on either arm.

But after brother Bob's nervous breakdown,
the hero's arm would begin to fail,
he'd start to doubt himself,
the Kennedys and King would get shot,
and one night he'd get hammered by the Sox
in a playoff game, and his dames
would leave him drinking scotch
in a dive where some loser trumpeter
is coming off a nod into a vamp,
and the former ace begins to write
on napkins from the bar
the story of life's raw deal.

Broke Down House

For Jim

Who needs all eighty-eight keys
and four-part harmony
to bang out beloved songs?
Why, this old piano thunders through
our parents' fights, smothers
the rhythm of their making up.
You're quick into the downbeat,
that one about our broke down house's

roof that needs a-patchin',
windows stuffed with rags.

You dreamed a monster was gnawing
our house's foundation, the wind through
stucco holes made mournful mouth-harp tunes,
and the furnace blew cold.
The plumbing, like our mother
humming sentimental strains,
clung to the past. You woke
to moans and squeaking bedsprings
from our parents' room.

We cringe as neighbors cock their ears
when they renew their war,
but the shouting goes unheard
when you belt out with your brother,

Ain't gonna fix them wobbly floorboards,
Ain't gonna oil that cellar door,

laying down those chords so hard
dust motes roil in the beam
streaming through the windowpane.

Neptune Festival

For Gary Levering (1939-2014)

Before Gary passed he came out of the dark
and claimed he would bring Dolphy back
to squawk him a sax requiem.

We used to wink at his manic antics,
toast his Seahawks in his box seats,
sign for his gifts of salmon on ice.

Now at night his voice like a small,
injured whale; sad noises turning
to the fevered speech of a magnate

who hosted presidents, survived
ten tiger-doctor surgeries, surfaced
from dolor's Mariana Trench.

So what have you done, my brother demands
in my dream, *to launch the Neptune Festival?*
He will pay all, but I am urged to marshal

the floats and ferry rides; organize
diving for pearls, pontoon golf, trident twirls;
order caviar platters, bikini babes, shark cages,

tuba solos, steamboat sex with kettle drums.
And patch the dolphin aquarium,
then the hole in my yacht, through which Gary,

despairing once more, has already plunged,
hugging the anchor, whose chain clatters
paying out from its coil toward ocean floor.

Lament from the Black Swamp

Woke up and threw off the covers
sweating with the ague and hungover.
Then I shivered when I was told
Juan Sada had been found
in a drainage ditch drowned.

At least the rain that stranded us
beat down the damn mosquitoes
though we were stuck with our guilt
staring from the porch
as the gutters overflowed.

Comes back round like a bluegrass tune
how his girl had snubbed him
and none would fiddle with him
and he'd spun out leaving the party
smashed and downcast.

Wish I could hear him again
trill the mandolin on *Ripple,*
pick the banjo on *Desperado.*
And oh how he sang high harmony.

That night in bed I'd slapped my ear
trying to hit a mosquito
that might have been his tires
whining on wet pavement.

The Choir of Youthful Suicides

A neighbor boy has knelt in the culvert
with his father's pistol
and swallowed a world war.

He joins the choir
beside the one with rope burns
on his neck, bulging eyes,

and a permanent erection.
They move their mouths
like fish in an aquarium

without a sound,
synching a song of confidence
that could never be sung in their lives.

They mime their demise —
one girl pours pills into her hand,
another saws across her wrists,

the new recruit opens wide
for the barrel of his father's gun.
As they silently chant

their litany of rejections,
we want to believe
what we hear is heavenly.

They assume that repetition
will make them be heard
as they lean toward the glass

between our worlds
mouthing the words *Do you miss me?*
But the only sounds we hear

are the fire hose
flushing the gore from the culvert
and the wailing from next door.

Hymn

Years unsung, it stirs inside,
turning through its verses
as I search the churchyard hours
for my grandparents' graves.
There is power, power, wonder working...

The yew that had marked their places
under snowfall or peony bloom
had been removed to hasten the mower.
...power in the blood of the Lamb.
There is power, power...

This hymn's unbidden chorus
restores my smallness in a pew
in a hand-me-down suit,
the tight, rote politeness,
standing for the organ's surge.

From a grandmother interred
with her hymnal,
from the child I was denied,
comes the creed I would suppress
along with the urge to hum

...power in the precious blood of the Lamb.

After Hours

The world's wares are locked behind grates
and bathed in blues.
Under tables stacked with chairs

sweeps a broom, sweeps a broom.
Laughter scatters into night air.
Through a second-story window waft

a keyboard's blurry voicing
and warbling sax.
The last electric bus crackles back

to the terminal.
From a dripping tunnel
echoes a woman singing scat.

Shoe soles scrape past glitter of glass
and eyes of a raccoon.
Around the corner comes

the thrumming of a sidewalk jam.
Drumsticks strike an overturned can.
Horns exclaim the chorus.

Ear Worm

I picture one inside the brain
like those engravings of leviathan
thrashing in briny swells,
more serpent or *wyrm* than whale.

When one surfaces, it seems
it has been playing in my background
long before I noticed.
Take this *Requiem,* which has been ringing
in one or another mortal's head
since the dying maestro
penned it three centuries ago.

Ahoy, here's another,
this resuscitated ditty
arresting my internal ear,
The Bristol Stomp, as fatuous
as it is implacable,
no matter how I strive
to dismiss it. Over and over,
the Bristol kids persist,
the same four chords,
the same inane lyrics.

Yesterday the augmented scale
of Oliver Nelson's *Stolen Moments*
wove through my trellis-mending,
but today, as I lean into sourdough,
Mozart's basset horns and chorus
commandeer my interior,
accompany my kneading
and dough's rising, the enthrallment
of its aroma bringing back
my grandmother's baking,
her rousing *Oklahoma!*,
and the sad strains of her senile demise.

Stirring in my aural lobes again
is Amadeus' solemn *Sanctus*
like a blue whale intoning
deep inside the ocean's folds.

In ***Barrelhouses,*** "Pinetop's Boogie-Woogie" refers to Pinetop Perkins, "Black Wolf Blues" is attributed to Champion Jack Dupree, and "All My Money's Gone" was recorded by Henry Townsend.

In ***Coltrane's God Admonishes,*** "Naima," "A Love Supreme," "Alabama," and "Blue Train" were written by John Coltrane. Jazz musicians noted in the poem who influenced Coltrane were Charlie Parker ("Bird"), Pharaoh Sanders, and Thelonious Monk.

In ***This is Not a Song I Used to Know,*** "In the Heart of the Heart Country" is by Fire Town. "Wildwood Flower" is best known for the Carter Family's version.

A Night in Tunisia is for reeds-man Greg Abate and keyboardist John Rangel. "Scrapple from the Apple" is by Charlie Parker; "Perdido" is by Juan Tido, famously recorded with Duke Ellington's band.

Grandpa weaves the author's paternal grandfather's biography with an account in Woody Guthrie's autobiography, *Bound for Glory*. The epigraph is a traditional folk song refrain used by Guthrie and others.

The stunning drummers mentioned besides John Trentacosta in ***Talking to the Octopus*** are the legendary Gene Krupa and the Panamanian kit-wizard Billy Cobham.

Cajón Maestro is for the Peruvian percussionist Freddy "Huevito" Lobatón.

After being discovered by an ethnomusicologist, the Malawi Mouse Boys in ***Yoga Teacher in Lilongwe Traffic*** now perform concerts on international tours.

Broke Down House was partly inspired by a song popularized by Rosemary Clooney.

In ***Neptune Festival***, Gary's resurrection of bop musician Eric Dolphy (1928-1964) was presumably to add the multi-reed player's wide range of quirky, often animal-like horn sounds to Gary's manic memorial party.

A large swath of present-day northwest Ohio was known as The Great Black Swamp (***Lament from the Black Swamp***). Settlers there were beset by mosquitoes, vectors of a malaria-like illness, "ague." Despite thousands of miles of drainage ditches, when it rains, the land reverts to swamp.

"Power in the Blood" in ***Hymn*** was written by Lewis E. Jones (1865-1936). Thanks to Stephen Bunch who helped this poem to realization.

Ear Worm uses "wyrm," an Old English term meaning "serpentine dragon." The Dovells sang "The Bristol Stomp."

This book is set in Palatino,
a 20th century font designed by Hermann Zapf,
based on the humanist typefaces of the Italian
Renaissance and named for the 16th century
Italian master of calligraphy, Giambattista Palatino.